The BDSM Contract Book

Michelle Fegatofi

Other works by Michelle Fegatofi:

BDSM Basics for Beginners – A Guide for Dominants and Submissive's Starting to Explore the Lifestyle

Unveiled – The Secret Submissive Within

BDSM Basics for Submissives – Dealing with the Mental and Emotional Side of Submission

BDSM Limits Worksheet (Free Download from Lu-lu.com/spotlight/MichelleFegatofi)

To find Michelle on the web, visit www.about.me/MichelleFegatofi to find out which sites she's on.

First Printing: 2015

ISBN 978-1-329-39440-7

BDSM Unveiled
Inquires: bdsmunveiled@gmail.com
www.bdsmunveiled.com

Dedication

To my Padrone Marco, without whom I would not have the courage or patience to pursue my dream of writing. Thank you for all of your support and love.
I would like to thank all of my readers and followers that have made it possible for me to do what I love, helping others understand the wonderful BDSM Lifestyle more in depth.

Acknowledgements

I would like to give a special thank you to a person that has become a dear friend and staunch supporter of my work. Ms. Sharon Charles, you are a wealth of knowledge. You see situations from different perspectives and have given me much food for thought. Thank you for your proof reading the earliest edition and for all of the suggestions on improvements you made. Most of all, thanks for being you and for your friendship.

Thank you to my Padrone Marco Belcastro Bara for all of the ideas he has given to me as well as the final editing for the book.

Contents

Introduction

This book is a guide to writing a non-legally binding contract between consenting adults. It will outline what each partner agrees to in their BDSM based relationship, covering all dynamics.

All contracts below should be altered to suit your own personal situation by changing titles, gender roles, deleting/adding rules, protocols, expectations, punishments, training, and all limits.

Although the contract forms are written for one Dominant and one submissive, this can also be altered to suit each individual relationship situation.

NOTICE: THE CONTRACTS CONTAINED WITHIN ARE IN NO WAY LEGALLY BINDING. THEY CAN NOT BE USED IN ANY LEGAL SITUATION. THE CONTRACTS ARE MEANT AS GUIDELINES FOR PEOPLE WHO PARTICIPATE IN BDSM RELATIONSHIPS OR ACTIVITIES. THEY DEFINE ROLES AND RESPONSIBILITIES AS WELL AS PROVIDE WRITTEN CONSENT TO WHATEVER ACTIVITIES ARE DOCUMENTED WITHIN EACH INDIVIDUAL CONTRACT.

Chapter 1: What is a BDSM Contract?

Usually a contract is a written agreement between the Dominant and submissive in a 24/7 relationship, but can also be used by those in training or couples that have regular play dates. It acts as the formal consent to the power exchange that takes place when in a BDSM role.

Some contracts are very formal and will detail exactly what is expected and can run for multiple pages. Others are as brief as a single paragraph. Either way, a contract is derived by negotiation on the part of all people involved in the relationship/play scene.

BDSM partners consider the Lifestyle contract to be equal in moral obligations as a marriage contract is. As such, constructing a proper contract is very much like writing a pre-nuptial agreement.

Here are some things you need to know before signing such a contract:

A slave contract is a non-legal document.
Although the contract is meaningful to the Dominant and his submissive, such a contract is not legally binding due to the fact that it is actually illegal to own another person and most slave contracts mention the word ownership in describing the relationship.

A BDSM contract is drawn up by the Dominant and presented to his submissive to sign.
Usually, a Dominant will allow his submissive to read the contract ahead of time and ask if she has any input or something she would like to include/exclude in the contract. If she does and the Dominant agrees, he will add/delete it to/from the contract.

Length of commitment varies.

Contracts vary in regard to the length of commitment pledged. While some Dominants may require a submissive to sign a lifetime agreement, other Dominants may ask for a six month or year long commitment. At the end of that time period, the submissive will have the choice to sign a renewal contract or to opt out of the relationship.

A slave contract signifies ownership.
Although the contract is not legally binding, it signifies a degree of ownership. Sometimes the ownership may be limited to sexual ownership. Sometimes it may mean complete ownership. This will depend on the couple and their preferences. It is very binding within the confines of the relationship and should not be entered into lightly.

Things to include in a BDSM contract.
A contract can include things such as expectations, training, rewards, punishments, protocols, rituals, and grounds for termination of the contract. Be sure and review the contract carefully, for what is in it will set the course of your relationship. Just as a couple who enters into marriage, you must have similar goals and expectations in regard to the relationship. Signing the contract means that you are agreeing to everything in it.

Don't be afraid to ask questions.
It is important that you feel free to ask questions before signing the contract. Submissives need to voice any fears or hesitations to the Dominant, and he needs to be open enough to listen to those fears and hesitations. If he is not open to hearing them, this should be the submissive's first clue to run in the opposite direction. It is also important for a Dominant to voice any concerns he may have to his submissive. If he senses any doubt or hesitation, it is vital for him to ask her about it, encouraging her to be open and honest with him.

Do not rush into signing a contract.

Although a contract can be an agreement between casual play partners or for a long term relationship, it is meant to signify a willingness to commit to a relationship for a certain amount of time. Take your time in getting to know one another before making the decision to make such a commitment.

Chapter 2: Rules, Rituals and Protocols

During your time with your Dominant, you will be expected to follow certain rules, protocols and rituals. Although they may change or evolve over time, as many of them as possible should be written into the initial contract.

A Protocol is how a Dominant and submissive interact with one another. Some examples of protocol would be how a sub greets a Dominant at a party, how they are dressed and greeting their Dom when they get home from work.

The D/s lifestyle has various situations which can involve different levels of protocol, for example an informal night at home might be low protocol, having D/s guests for dinner maybe medium protocol, but a formal D/s dinner would be high protocol.

Low protocol is easy going and usual in most informal situations or casual stay at home nights. It is also what many D/s couples use if they are in "vanilla situations" such as family get togethers, where not everyone is aware of the lifestyle. Only to the practiced eye, is the subtle D/s interaction noticeable, but there is no doubt in the submissive's mind that it is there.

Medium protocol is a step up from low protocol. It is still fairly easy going but there is a bit of an edge to things, and the submissive is a little more aware of his/her behavior. It may involve things such as wearing a collar at the table for the evening, being mindful and respectful to whomever is around you, but being able to speak fairly freely, as long as you are respectful.

If a submissive or slave is put on high protocol, she/he is instructed to behave in a certain manner befitting a high protocol situation - she/he would have certain rules to follow. High protocol usually means all focus is on the Dominant, and no communication with anyone else, unless directed, is allowed. The submissive would keep eyes lowered and be quiet at all times, and remain in whatever position or place she/ he has been instructed to stay in.

A ritual is a sequence of actions / words / gestures that are performed the same exact way for one specific purpose. An example could be having a meditation ritual. Dressing a certain way, setting up a place to meditate a certain way, and the actual act of meditation.

Rules are the specific guidelines a submissive/slave lives by. They are set by the Dominant and can govern everything from what clothes to wear to a set exercise routine.

Common Rules Submissives/Slaves Use -

- Above all else, the primary focus is to please your Master, whether you are in His presence or not. He knows what is best for you.
- Worship your Master.
- Worship your Master's body.
- The power of your Master's will, thoughts of Him or the hearing of His voice, gives you strength.
- To receive pleasure, you must earn it.
- Trust your Master: your safety, as well as your emotional, psychological, social, sexual, and physical health are his utmost priority.
- You are an object of great value - an instrument Master will use to draw out His pleasures.
- You will ask your Master for permission to satisfy whatever needs you have before acting on it.
- Your body and mind are the property of your Master.
- Always give thanks to your Master for all you are given, immediately after receiving whatever He has given you, for such things are gifts or privileges granted to you by Him.
- You must be both specific and explicit in your speech.
- Never hesitate when responding to your Master. Your complete focus is important to your continued growth.
- Thank your Master for the discipline and punishments you receive, repeating the reason you were punished.

- You are always submissive to your Master whether He is present or not, ready to please Him at any time, in any place, under any circumstances, regardless of who may be present. Trust your Master to keep you safe.
- All choices shall be based upon whether or not they will please Master.
- When you are not in the presence of Master and have choices to make, always stay within the boundaries and guidance He has allowed when making decisions.
- Wear the collar of your Master with pride, for it signifies His ownership of you and your devotion to Him.
- Worship your Master's cock when given the opportunity, whether it is hard or soft, for pleasing Him and making Him happy is the main goal. It will make you feel good to do so.
- Your greatest satisfaction is realized when you know you have pleased your Master.
- There can be no greater pain or suffering you will feel than when Master is not pleased with you. Naturally, you may feel depressed, saddened, empty, and lost. Hope He will show His mercy and provide the guidance you will need to get back on track and be forgiven.
- Your submission should be a natural internal feeling. It is a very powerful force inside you that only a respectful and knowledgeable Master can recognize, control and manage. He understands how your nature influences your behavior. He, too, manages and controls His own naturally dominate state, through sharing a power exchange between you, bonding you tightly to Him.
- Fear nothing, for your Master is always with you and will take care of you.
- Never hesitate in your obedience to your Master.
- Choose to willingly be treated as your Master's property - as long as such treatment is safe and legal.

- When Master feels you are ready and your relationship has progressed to a lifelong commitment, be prepared to receive His unique and permanent mark of ownership upon your body, in a place of His choosing, whether it be a piercing, a tattoo or a branding.
- Remember you are your Master's greatest treasure.
- Learn all the positions Master wants to teach you to the best of your abilities and be prepared to take such positions when required.
- Confess everything to your Master, even when you have been naughty, so that He may decide if such violations require discipline or punishment. Accept whatever decisions He makes by thanking Him for His choice. Focus on how sorry you are for not behaving in the way in which you were taught and for the defilement you brought to yourself and to Him with the unacceptable act which has displeased Him.
- You are a slave - of worth and value to any Master who would find you useful. Your role has been clearly defined by your true nature, enhanced through the teachings of your Master, and will be practiced every day to the continued pleasure of your Master.
- You have much to learn in order to become a well-trained and well-behaved slave.
- Endure whatever discipline or punishment Master gives you in order to become a better slave for Him.
- Never think of yourself as a weak person, because it takes a strong one to commit to the drive inside yourself, to serve, to obey and to please a Master.
- Strive to continue to be a devoted slave, of good rapport to a Master who truly understands your needs in relationship to His own.
- Give all that you are to a Master in order to become free. For in submission, you find ultimate freedom.
- Never show disrespect towards your Master in any way - no matter where you are - in his presence or not.

- Only in complete submission you can realize the depth of the love you have for Him, your Master.
- Always be attentive to the needs of your Master and be ready to respond to them to the best of your abilities.
- You are allowed to suggest ways to further your training or use by verbally addressing them your Master when the timing is right.
- Always respond fully, both physically and verbally, to whatever Master does with you. Emotional and physical responses are important to Him. Never hold back any part of your display, regardless of how intense they may be, unless restricted to do so.
- You are a sexual and sensual being.
- Never be passive in serving your Master. Aggressively participate in your exchange with Him.

Examples of Protocols for Submissives/Slaves:

At home with no one else present -

- You should always remove your clothing as soon as you get home, unless Master/ Mistress have laid out clothing for you to wear.
- You should fold clothes neatly or place them in the laundry whenever you get undressed.
- You are to kneel in present posture whenever the Master/ Mistress is due to arrive and wait quietly.
- Whenever the Master/ Mistress is present in a room, you must ask permission to enter.
- You will kneel in the room until the Master/ Mistress gives permission that you may move or proceed with cleaning.
- You will wear, and gratefully accept, any toys the Master/ Mistress choose to insert or adorn you with in any circumstance.
- You will not speak unless spoken to. Request an opportunity to speak, if there is something pressing to discuss during those periods of time when the Master/ Mistress commands silence.
- You may request an opportunity to serve your Dominant.
- You will always thank your Master/ Mistress for an opportunity to serve, whether it was doing a chore or being flogged.
- You will keep your eyes averted unless it is the wish of the Master/ Mistress to have you look them in the eyes.
- You will address the Master/ Mistress not by their first name, but by the title preferred by that Dominant.

In public and at home with others present -

- You will receive visitors at the door with whatever clothing the Master or Mistress commanded.
- You will greet visitors in whatever manner the Master/ Mistress commands - this may include just taking coats and putting them away, kissing the hand of the guest or kneeling in front of them.

- You will not refer to anyone using his or her first name. You will use the title Sir or Ma'am combined with their name to differentiate and to make sure that you always remember your place.
- You will serve every person with food and drinks as requested, kneeling to each as the food or drinks are presented.
- You will not use furniture and will kneel on the floor until your services are required.
- You will not speak unless spoken to.
- You will remain attentive to make sure that no one has to ask for additional food or drink. You should be ready before the command is issued.
- You must use high protocol when commanded to do so. This means that you will not use first person language when referring to yourself and will address everyone present with the title each Dominant prefers.

Chapter 3: Submissive Training

During your contract negotiations, your Dominant will most likely add training expectations and goals that he will expect you to fulfill during your contract period. You need to make sure that you are comfortable with the training specified in the contract and that you are physically and mentally able to complete that training. If for some reason you are uncomfortable or think you are incapable of performing a certain type of training session, you have to be honest and upfront with your Dominant and give them valid reasons for your concerns.

Training Methods

Discipline and punishment:
Discipline and punishment is used to correct conscious as well as unconscious mistakes made by a slave or submissive in the training process. These tools are also used to help prevent any recurrences of the mistakes made by the slave or submissive. It can take various forms from physical labor or punishment, time in a corner, or being ignored.

Written Assignments:
Written assignments help both parties to get to know each other and will help the Dominant understand the submissive's personal and training needs more effectively. They are also a tool to help the submissive grow and to help both partners communicate more effectively. Written assignments also serve as a type of punishment to help a submissive remember requirements more effectively.

Outside training courses:
Courses like etiquette, cooking, tea service, make up application, massage etc. can be incorporated into an effective training course. Training needs will be identified during the negotiation process and should become clear during the training process. The Dominant must make sure that the goals are set properly, a schedule is followed and that follow up testing occurs as the submissive progresses through the course.

Bondage:
Tying up a submissive can help them move into subspace and a type of meditation. The Dominant can specify the goal of alone time for a submissive and test him or her after the period of meditation to see what insights the submissive has gained. The Dominant may also use floggers, paddles, canes, whips etc. to help a submissive achieve certain training goals - remember this is not the discipline and punishment we were talking about before.

Regular testing:
Testing the submissive or slave regularly during the training process will help to measure the achievement of set goals within the scheduled training period. The Dominant will not notify the submissive before a skill is tested but will communicate the results to the submissive after the test. Rewards should be given for good performance and discipline for weak performance

Positions and Voice Training:
These are the positions and voice commands your Dominant will teach you. These positions ensure that you are constantly in submissive/slave mode and remember your place during and after the training. It is one of the first things you will learn during training.

Areas of Training (unless listed under Hard Limits)

- Physical training - developing specific muscles, movements, postures, moving between poses, holding positions, increasing flexibility, adapting certain yoga postures for submissive effect.
- Sexual training - increasing arousal, becoming sexual in new ways, overcoming sexual blocks, erotic movement, dance, striptease, pole dance, controlling masturbation, orgasm restriction, overcoming shame about body and sexuality.

- Emotional training - overcoming unhelpful emotions, control over emotional expression, openness, journal keeping, overcoming fear, guilt, shame, dishonesty, possessiveness, materialism, stubbornness, resistance, surliness, egotism. Accepting humiliation, overcoming expectations, entitlement feelings, and resentment at unfairness.
- Mental training - Training of the will, persistence, obedience, determination, sticking to a task, problem solving.
- Skills training - examples include cooking, making own punishment implements & restraints, jewelry, singing, dancing, playing a musical instrument, painting, poetry.
- Verbal training - control of speech, use or restriction of certain words, rule of silence, speaking more slowly, conciseness, expressing key points with clarity, listening skills.
- Non-verbal training - control of body language, using the body to communicate, reading body language of others.
- Rituals - disrupting old habits and creating new ones.

Chapter 4: Negotiating Punishments

Every BDSM relationship is different, so remember, thoughts on punishments differ greatly from couple to couple. Culture, age, and personality all play into the way people see punishment. Below is a compilation of my personal views and those I have gathered over the years from other sources.

Punishment should only be given if a sub deliberately starts or causes trouble or breaks rules that were put in place for her safety. Punishment should not be given out all the time because it can have lasting effects on the sub's mental and emotional wellbeing. If you punish a sub for every slight infraction, it can start to make that sub feel worthless instead of having the opposite effect of making them perform better.

For the "to punish or not to punish" question, that is entirely up to the Dominant. If you know your sub has difficulties when performing certain tasks for you but she does perform them to the best of her ability, I would recommend that you remain understanding and encourage her to keep trying her best. If you punish her for not being able to perform perfectly on the first or even third try, but you see that she has improved, even slightly, then punishing her for not being perfect will just add to the aggravation and disappointment she already feels inside herself.

As a true submissive, she will most likely be feeling like she has let her Dominant down by not performing the task perfectly as he asked. I will use myself as an example for this. I have epilepsy and it does have a long lasting effect on my memory. There are days when I am very slow and something as routine as making coffee is difficult for me to remember.

My Padrone knows me so well and is so in tune with me that he recognizes when I am in one of these 'zones'. I have given him a cup of hot water before because I forgot to add the actual coffee to the machine! He did not punish me or yell, he actually made me feel better because I felt really stupid and was very hard on myself. He helped me laugh about it, went with me back to the machine and told me step by step what to do so that I was able to finish the task and regain some of my self-confidence. There are many other examples and stories I could share, but you can see what I mean when I say the punishment should fit the circumstances.

If you give your sub a task like having dinner on the table when you get home from work and you find a sandwich when you were expecting a four course meal, you have to stop and think about the actual wording of the order. Did you just tell her to 'have dinner ready and on the table' by the time you get home? Or did you say 'I want steak and mashed potatoes on the table' by the time you get home? When you give an order or task, ensure you do so in precise wording that is not vague, so there can be no misunderstandings. The vaguer you are with a task or command, the more room for interpretation there is for the sub.

If your sub tends to be lazy and take the easiest way out when left with a vague order, I suggest you give her very precise orders where there is little or no room for interpretation. If she tends to be an overachiever or always exceeds your vague orders, then you are safe to continue, as you know she will always meet and exceed your commands.

There are subs that crave punishment because of the attention it gives them from the Dominant. These types of submissives will constantly do things to make their Dominant angry just to receive punishment. If you have one of these subs, I suggest you re-evaluate your relationship and how your punishment system works.

There are many different forms of punishment for both real life and cyber submissives. The main thing to remember is the reason for the punishment. When given, it should be done in a way to ensure the sub understands deeply why she is being punished. It should also be done in some form or way that the submissive does not like.

As forms of punishments, a Dominant may ground, isolate, assign essays or line writing, time outs, have the slave kneel on the ice/rice/pebbles, control what the sub eats, where they sleep, where they sit, or institute speech restrictions. There are many more forms of punishment, but these are the most widely used.

If you notice, I left out spanking and flogging as many subs are masochists and see these as a form of reward instead. The more they are spanked/flogged, the more they will continue to act out.

Specific Unpleasant Chore
This can include things such as cleaning the stove, cleaning blinds and windows, scrubbing the floor with a toothbrush, detailing a car, etc. The Dominant can make a list of chores and rotate through them to avoid re-cleaning a recently cleaned item. Chores assigned as punishments should not include chores that are part of the submissives normal duties. It is important to distinguish normal chores from '"punishment chores" or the submissive may start to view all chores as punishment

Sleeping on the Floor (or somewhere other than normal sleep arrangements)
This punishment can be effective for dealing with a submissive that has become too vanilla in manners. Because of social conditioning this punishment tends to stress the position of the submissive relative to the Dominant.

Standing in a Corner

This is an old standard. It gives the submissive time to think about the infraction. The length of time can vary from a few minutes to an hour or more. It is suggested that the Dominant try this punishment for themselves, to get a sense of how difficult this punishment may or may not be for the length of time in question.

Writing Assignments of Some Specific Length
This punishment is helpful when the Dominant wants the submissive to think about or research a subject. It is recommended that this punishment be used intermittently rather than regularly to keep the act of writing from taking on a negative connotation.

Kneeling On a Hard Surface
This is a classic punishment that combines giving the submissive time to think about the infraction with mild physical discomfort. If the length of time to kneel will exceed 20 minutes, it is recommended that a full 5 minute break be given after every 20 minutes. Kneeling for too long on a hard surface can cause nerve damage. It is also good to keep in mind that some submissives may not be able to kneel 20 minutes because of physical conditions. It may be that some submissives need to do cycles of 10 minutes of kneeling and 5 minutes of rest.

Kneeling On Uncooked Rice
Kneeling on a hard surface can be made more severe by dropping a handful of uncooked rice on the floor where the submissive is going to kneel. Once the time period is done, the submissive can be instructed to clean up the rice as part of bringing the punishment to a close. This is another punishment where it's suggested the Dominant try it for themselves to get a feel of the punishment. The same cautions and time limits apply to this as when kneeling without the rice. The Dominant should also be aware that the rice sometimes causes marking of the skin. Lastly, do not use instant rice as it crumbles and defeats the purpose of using rice.

Food Restrictions

Obviously some common sense is required with using food restrictions as punishment. Being sent to bed without dinner is certainly not going to cause a healthy individual any harm. However, denying a diabetic food after they took their insulin could result in death. One suggested way to use food restrictions is to deny the submissive sweets for a period of time (days/weeks) as a punishment.

Restriction of Computer, TV Privileges, Etc.
Restriction of recreational access to things such as the computer or TV can be useful motivators when they can be enforced. The restriction can be total, where the submissive is not allowed any access to the items, or it can be limited to a certain amount of time. There is a wide range of options under this heading.

Cold Shower
A brief cold shower can be used as a rather impressive punishment. There are several points to keep in mind when using this as a punishment. First, tap water varies in temperature depending on the time of year. A small difference in temperature makes a huge difference in the severity of the punishment. Next, it is important to define what is meant by "short". Less than 5 minutes is generally quite safe for any fit person; however, an unexpected burst of cold water for 30 seconds can be shocking. This is another 'try it before you use it' type of punishment.

Send the Submissive to a Room by Themselves
This one generally speaks for itself. It gives time for calming down and for reflecting. This is often a good choice when the Dom wants to avoid adding stress to a situation.

Grounding
Being restricted to home can be a relatively effective and low stress punishment. External factors greatly affect the harshness of being restricted to home. This means that the same punishment is more or less severe depending on what else is going on in the submissive's life at the time. Being restricted when one has already bought tickets to a concert is more significant than being restricted when one has no plans.

Speech Restrictions

Speech restrictions can range from requiring the submissive to speak in third person to requiring the submissive to not speak at all for a period of time. When silence is used as a punishment it is helpful to have the submissive carry around a notebook and pen so they can convey necessary information. Requiring a submissive to speak in third person is an effective way to make the submissive aware of self-centered behavior. Many times a submissive may not be aware of how often they refer to their own opinions and desires in casual speech.

Public Apology

Apologizing in a public forum stresses humility. The Dominant must carefully consider the reaction of those who are going to hear the apology.

Financial Penalties - Allowance Restrictions

If the Dominant controls the finances in the relationship, restricting money can be used as a punishment. This is the same as a parent withholding allowance and generally works best over shorter terms such as a week to a month. When it becomes longer than a month, the punishment starts to become the norm.

Lecture

A good old-fashioned lecture can be an effective punishment. The lecture should include what specifically was wrong with the submissive's behavior and why it was wrong. The lecture should also include what the submissive should have done under the circumstance and why. If the submissive is required to maintain a physically stressful position during the lecture (such as kneeling) then the Dominant must also keep in mind cautions associated with the physical position such as time limits.

Dominant Expressing Anger

As odd as it may sound to some, the simple expression that the Dominant is angry at the submissive often carries a fair amount of punishment value. However, a fair number of submissives are inclined to view criticism and/or the expression of anger as an indication that the Dominant does not care about them. This can be a nightmare of a problem and it is one that Dominants should always keep in mind.

Silence, or ignoring a submissive for punishment, is considered by some Dominants as an acceptable form of punishment. But a growing movement in many BDSM circles considers this to be a form of emotional abuse. A Dominant should know that a submissive will already punish themselves harsher and longer than their Dominant will if they make mistakes. Pleasing a Dominant and having him/her show pride in their submissive is one of the greatest pleasures a sub receives. If the Dominant ignores the sub to teach them a lesson, it only teaches them to feel alone, stupid and unworthy on top of whatever mental punishment they usually inflict on themselves.

Always keep safety in mind, as well as the purpose of the punishment. Make sure the punishment fits the crime. It is a punishment that the sub does not like and the lesson will be learned without lasting mental, emotional, or physical harm.

Ensure that whatever punishment is given, it is not listed as a Hard Limit.

Chapter 5: Soft and Hard Limits

Limits encompass everything (mentally, physically, and emotionally) that you will and will not allow in a BDSM relationship.

If you are at a point where you are thinking of entering into a BDSM contract with someone, you have to have all of your limits in place and make sure they will be honored by your Dominant. Write three different lists: one that contains things that are permissible, one that contains things that you may want to try but are scared to, and one that contains items that are absolutely off limits, no matter what your Dominant says or does.

Hard Limits
Something that must not be done. Violating a hard limit is often considered just cause for ending a scene or even a relationship.

NEVER say you don't have limits unless you are with a Dominant that has the exact same morals as you do or you can trust to not take you into places that you do not want to go. If you don't have well defined limits, this could become a problem if you do not know each other inside and out.

Soft Limits
Something that someone will do only in special circumstances or when highly aroused.

Below is a list of different activities you should consider adding to your contract as a hard or soft limit if you choose to. This list should be used as a guideline only and remember that it does not cover every possible activity.

- Anal Play
  Acts in which the anus is involved.
- Beating (General)
  Acts in which one partner is beaten.

- Beating - Canes
  Acts in which one partner is beaten with a cane.
- Beating - Crops
  Acts in which one partner is beaten with a crop.
- Beating - Floggers
  Acts in which one partner is beaten with a flogger.
- Beating - Hairbrushes
  Acts in which one partner is beaten with a hairbrush.
- Beating - Hard
  Acts in which one partner is beaten hard.
- Beating - Paddles
  Acts in which one partner is beaten with a paddle.
- Beating - Soft
  Acts in which one partner is beaten softly.
- Beating - Spanking
  Acts in which one partner is beaten with a hand.
- Beating - Straps
  Acts in which one partner is beaten with a strap.
- Beating - Whips
  Acts in which one partner is beaten with a whip.
- Beating Location - Back
  Beating based acts that focus on the back as a target.
- Beating Location - Bottom
  Beating based acts that focus on the bottom as a target.
- Beating Location - Chest
  Beating based acts that focus on the chest or breasts as a target.
- Beating Location - Feet
  Beating based acts that focus on the feet (usually the soles) as a target.
- Beating Location - Genitals
  Beating based acts that focus on the genitals as a target.
- Beating Location - Legs
  Beating based acts that focus on the legs as a target.
- Bestiality
  Sex with animals.

- Biting
  Acts involving one partner biting the other.
- Blindfolds
  Acts in which blindfolds are placed over one partner's eyes to remove that sense (and often heighten others).
- Body Modification - Branding
  Burning the body, often with a specific design, to leave a permanent mark or scar.
- Body Modification - Piercing, Permanent
  Putting an object through a part of the body for permanent adornment.
- Body Modification - Piercing, Play
  Exploring the concept of body piercing but in a manner that is temporary.
- Body Modification - Saline Injection
  Injecting saline in to a part of the body to temporarily engorge it.
- Body Modification - Scarification
  Deliberately causing scars, often through cutting the skin, for adornment.
- Body Modification - Tattooing
  Adorning the body by permanently applying ink under the skin.
- Bondage (General)
  Binding or restricting some or all of the body.
- Bondage - Breast
  Binding or restricting the breasts.
- Bondage - Cuffs
  Binding or restricting the body (usually the wrists) with [hand]cuffs.
- Bondage - Genital
  Binding or restricting the genitals. (Chastity Belt / Cock Cage)
- Bondage - Heavy
  Heavily binding or restricting the body, usually to the point where no, or next-to no, movement is possible.
- Bondage - Intricate
  Intricately binding or restricting some or all of the body.
- Bondage - Light

Lightly binding or restricting the body. Usually more symbolic than actually restrictive.

- Bondage - Locks
  Bondage that involves locks and keys.
- Bondage - Prolonged
  Binding or restricting some or all of the body for prolonged periods of time.
- Bondage - Sleeves, Arm
  Restricting the movement of the arms by placing them in a confining sleeve.
- Bondage - Sleeves, Leg
  Restricting the movement of the legs by placing them in a confining sleeve.
- Bondage - Spreader Bars
  Restricting the movement of the legs by connecting them to either end of a bar, usually forcing them open.
- Bondage - Stocks
  Restricting movement by placing the wrists and neck (though may involve ankles) through a set of stocks.
- Bondage - Strait Jackets
  Binding or restricting the torso and arms by placing them inside a strait jacket.
- Bondage - Suspension
  Binding or restricting someone so they are suspended above the ground.
- Bondage - Suspension, Inverted
  Binding or restricting someone so they are suspended above the ground, upside-down.
- Bondage - Whole Body
  Binding or restricting the whole body.
- Bondage Material - Chain
  Binding or restricting the body, or parts of, with chain.
- Bondage Material - Leather
  Binding or restricting the body, or parts of, with leather.
- Bondage Material - Rope

Binding or restricting the body, or parts of, with rope.
- Bondage Material - Plastic Wrap
Binding or restricting the body, or parts of, with plastic cling film.
- Bondage Material - Scarves
Binding or restricting the body, or parts of, with [usually silk] scarves.
- Bondage Material - Tape
Binding or restricting the body, or parts of, with [usually adhesive] tape.
- Breath Play
Also called Asphyxiation. Acts involving restricting or cutting off the supply of oxygen.
- Catheters
Inserting a tube in to the urethra to collect urine.
- Clothespins
Using clothespins to pinch parts of the body.
- Clothing - Chosen For
Having your clothing choices made for you, usually without the ability to appeal.
- Clothing - Corsets
Wearing corsets which control the shape of the waist and hips
- Clothing - Full Head Hoods
Wearing hoods that cover the entire head, leaving only small holes for vision, breathing, etc. (if even them).
- Clothing - Harnesses
Wearing clothing that harnesses the body without necessarily covering it.
- Clothing - High Heels
Wearing high-heeled shoes.
- Clothing - Lingerie
Wearing women's lingerie.
- Clothing - Masks
Wearing masks that cover the face.
- Clothing - Uniforms (General)
Wearing uniforms that have a given significance.

- Clothing - Uniforms, Military
  Wearing military uniforms.
- Clothing - Uniforms, School
  Wearing schoolgirl/schoolboy uniforms.
- Clothing Material - Leather
  Clothing made out of, or involving, leather.
- Clothing Material - Latex/PVC
  Clothing made out of, or involving, Latex/PVC.
- Clothing Material - Rubber
  Clothing made out of, or involving, rubber or latex.
- Clothing Material - Sheer
  Clothing made out of, or involving, sheer (transparent or translucent) material.
- Collars - Private
  Wearing a collar in private.
- Collars - Public
  Wearing a collar in public.
- Crawling
  The act of crawling on all fours to denote submission.
- Cutting
  Deliberately cutting the skin.
- Dilation - Anal
  Intentionally stretching the anus open.
- Dilation - Vaginal
  Intentionally stretching the vagina open.
- Discipline
  Submitting to, or receiving, the [often corporal] discipline of another.
- Drinking - Blood
  Drinking blood.
- Drinking - Semen
  Drinking semen.
- Drinking - Urine
  Drinking urine.
- Electricity
  Using electricity for sensation or pain.

- Enemas
  Applying liquid (traditionally warm water) into the lower intestine, via a tube. Often to induce uncontrolled, or hard to control, excretion.
- Examination - Physical
  Having your body physically examined and, often, appraised. Sometimes this includes medical examination role-plays though, here, that is listed as Role-play - Medical.
- Exhibitionism - Forced
  Exposing your body to others, nominally against your will, at the will of another.
- Exhibitionism - Voluntary
  Willingly exposing your body to others.
- Face Slapping
  Slapping the face, usually with an open hand, to cause pain or denote position.
- Fisting - Anal
  Placing an entire hand inside the anus.
- Fisting - Vaginal
  Placing an entire hand inside the vagina.
- Food - Chosen For
  Having your food choices made for you, usually without the ability to appeal.
- Food - From Body
  Eating food from another person's body. Either eating it directly from them or using them as a platter.
- Food - From Bowl
  Eating food directly from a bowl, like an animal such as a cat or dog.
- Food - From Hand
  Eating food directly from another person's hand.
- Gags (General)
  Devices used to limit, or prevent, verbal communication.
- Gags - Ball
  A type of gag that uses a ball to effectively block any verbal communication.
- Gags - Bit

A type of gag that uses a bar that goes across the mouth, much like a horse's "bit".

- Gags - Ring
  A type of gag that uses a ring to force the mouth open while providing complete access.
- Gags - Tape
  Using adhesive tape across the mouth to create a gag.
- Given Away (General)
  Being given, at a partner's whim, to another person, usually temporarily.
- Given Away - Auctions
  Being given to another person as the result of a [slave] auction.
- Given Away - Permanent
  Being given away, at a partner's whim, to another person, permanently.
- Hand Jobs
  Pleasuring someone else's genitals with your hand.
- Heterosexuality - Forced
  Sexual acts with members of the opposite sex, nominally against your will.
- Heterosexuality - Voluntary
  Sexual acts with members of the opposite sex, willingly.
- Homosexuality - Forced
  Sexual acts with members of the same sex, nominally against your will.
- Homosexuality - Voluntary
  Sexual acts with members of the same sex, willingly.
- Humiliation - Private
  Acts in which you are humiliated, degraded, or shamed, in a private setting.
- Humiliation - Public
  Acts in which you are humiliated, degraded, or shamed, in front of others.
- Humiliation - Verbal

Acts in which you are humiliated, degraded, or shamed, through either the words of someone else (such as name calling) or your own words.

- Including Others
  Acts in which other people, from outside your immediate relationship, are included.
- Kneeling
  The act of kneeling to denote submission.
- Leashes
  Wearing a leash, attached to a collar (or other convenient point).
- Lecturing
  An exposition of a given subject for the purpose of instruction or reprimand.
- Licking
  Using your tongue on another person's body [or, often, anything they require].
- Massage
  Rubbing another person's body for their relaxation.
- Masturbation - Forced
  Pleasuring your own genitals, with your hand, nominally against your will.
- Masturbation - Voluntary
  Pleasuring your own genitals, with your hand, willingly.
- Nipple Clamps
  Placing clamps on the nipples to cause pain.
- Nipple Play
  Acts that focus on the nipples.
- Nipple Weights
  Applying weights to the nipples to stretch them, generally to cause pain.
- Nudity - Forced
  Periods of time spent without clothing, nominally against you will.
- Nudity - Voluntary
  Periods of time spent without clothing.
- Orgasm - On Command

Having to orgasm on the command of another person.

- Orgasm Control
  Giving control of when and how orgasms are experienced - and when they are not - to another person.
- Orgasm Denial
  Losing the right to have orgasms for a [often protracted] period of time.
- Pain (General)
  Acts involving physical pain.
- Pain - Heavy
  Acts involving a very large degree of physical pain.
- Pain - Light
  Acts involving some physical pain, yet without too great an intensity - being more symbolic than serious.
- Phone Sex
  Having sexually explicit phone conversations, usually involving performing sexual acts at the same time.
- Rape - Fantasy
  Acts that explore being sexually used, nominally against your will, by another person.
- Rape - Fantasy, Gang
  Acts that explore being sexually used, nominally against your will, by more than one other person.
- Recorded Scenes - Photographs, Private
  Having photographs taken of you, either naked or indulging in a sexual act, for private viewing only.
- Recorded Scenes - Photographs, Shared
  Having photographs taken of you, either naked or indulging in a sexual act, to be shared with others.
- Recorded Scenes - Video, Private
  Having video taken of you, either naked or indulging in a sexual act, for private viewing only.
- Recorded Scenes - Video, Shared
  Having video taken of you, either naked or indulging in a sexual act, to be shared with others.

- Role-play (General)
  Scenes in which the participants take on and act out roles.
- Role-play - Age
  Scenes in which the participants take on and act out roles based on being a different age (such as babies or naughty young girls).
- Role-play - Education
  Scenes in which the participants take on and act out roles based on a scholastic teacher/student setting.
- Role-play - Interrogation
  Scenes in which the participants take on and act out roles based on interrogations where one person is the interrogator and the other the subject.
- Role-play - Kidnapping
  Scenes in which the participants take on and act out roles based on one partner being kidnapped.
- Role-play - Medical
  Scenes in which the participants take on and act out roles such as Doctor/Patient.
- Role-play - Pig
  Scenes in which the subject takes on and acts out a role based on being a pig.
- Role-play - Pony
  Scenes in which the subject takes on and acts out a role based on being a pony.
- Role-play - Prison
  Scenes in which the participants take on and act out roles based on the prison world such as Sadistic Jailer/Vulnerable Inmate
- Role-play - Puppy
  Scenes in which the subject takes on and acts out a role based on being a puppy or adult dog
- Role-play - Religious
  Scenes in which the participants take on and act out roles based on the religious world such as confessionals or Bishop/Nun.
- Role-play - Whore

Scenes in which the subject takes on and acts out a role based on being a male or female prostitute, selling themselves to another person for sex.

- Sensation Play (General)
  Acts involving the senses and strong sensations
- Sensation Play - Deprivation
  Acts involving depriving the subject of their senses (often to heighten the remaining ones).
- Sensation Play - Fire
  Acts involving the sensations and apprehensions caused by fire and heat.
- Sensation Play - Hair Pulling
  Acts involving the sensations and apprehensions caused by having hair pulled.
- Sensation Play - Hot Wax
  Acts involving the sensations and apprehensions caused by having hot candle wax dripped on to or applied to the body.
- Sensation Play - Ice
  Acts involving the sensations and apprehensions caused by using ice or other cold items on the body.
- Sensation Play - Needle
  Acts involving the sensations and apprehensions caused by using needles on the body, either scratching with them, or poking them.
- Sensation Play - Scratching
  Acts involving the sensations and apprehensions caused by being scratched.
- Sensation Play - Suction
  Acts involving the sensations and apprehensions caused by having suction applied to the body.
- Sensation Play - Teasing
  Acts involving the sensations and apprehensions caused by teasing the body.
- Sensation Play - Tickling
  Acts involving the sensations and apprehensions caused by tickling the body.

- Serving (General)
  Serving another person in specific ways, putting their pleasure ahead of your own. For example, a maid or a sexual servant.
- Serving - Art
  Serving another person, putting their pleasure ahead of your own, as a (usually immobile) piece of artwork such as a statue.
- Serving - Ashtray
  Serving another person, putting their pleasure ahead of your own, using a part of your body as a receptacle for their cigarette or cigar ash.
- Serving - Chauffer
  Serving another person, putting their pleasure ahead of your own, as their formal driver.
- Serving - Dancer
  Serving another person, putting their pleasure ahead of your own, as a dancer. For example, a belly dancer or stripper.
- Serving - Following Orders
  Serving another person, putting their pleasure ahead of your own, as they give you specific formal orders to follow.
- Serving - Forced
  Serving another person in specific ways, putting their pleasure ahead of your own, nominally forced against your will.
- Serving - Furniture
  Serving another person, putting their pleasure ahead of your own, as an immobile piece of furniture. For example, on all fours as a table or a footstool.
- Serving - Housework
  Serving another person, putting their pleasure ahead of your own, performing household chores.
- Serving - Maid
  Serving another person, putting their pleasure ahead of your own, as a maid. For example, serving tea while wearing a uniform.
- Serving - Sexually
  Serving another person, putting their pleasure ahead of your own, in whatever sexual way pleases them.

- Sex - Anal
  Sexual intercourse involving a penis entering your anus.
- Sex - Cunnilingus
  Sexually stimulating the vagina with a mouth/tongue.
- Sex - Denial
  Going without sex, or sexual gratification, often at another person's command.
- Sex - Fellatio
  Sexually stimulating the penis with a mouth/tongue.
- Sex - Group
  Sexual intercourse with more than one partner.
- Sex - Penetration, Double
  Sexual intercourse in which two orifices (mouth, vagina, anus) are filled.
- Sex - Penetration, Triple
  Sexual intercourse in which three orifices (mouth, vagina, anus) are filled.
- Sex - Rimming
  Sexually stimulating the anus with a mouth/tongue.
- Sex - Threesome
  Sexual intercourse with two other people.
- Sex - Vaginal
  Sexual intercourse involving a penis entering your vagina.
- Sex - Vanilla
  Traditional sexual intercourse, without involving any kinks.
- Sex Toys - Beads
  Having a string of connected beads (or balls) inserted in to your anus or vagina and then pulled out.
- Sex Toys - Butt Plugs
  Wearing a "plug" inserted in to your anus.
- Sex Toys - Dildos
  Using and/or being penetrated with a non-vibrating artificial phallus.
- Sex Toys - Eggs

Variously known as Ben-Wa Balls, Love Eggs, etc. Two balls made to be vaginally inserted which vibrate when you move or are battery powered to vibrate.
- Sex Toys - Public (Under Clothes)
Going out in public with a sex toy (such as a butt plug) in your body, under your clothing.
- Sex Toys - Strap On
Using and/or being penetrated with an artificial phallus that fastens about a partner's waist.
- Sex Toys - Vibrators
Using and/or being penetrated with a vibrating toy, usually an artificial phallus.
- Shaving - Body
Removing all traces of hair below the neck.
- Shaving - Genital
Removing all traces of hair from the genitals.
- Shaving - Genital, Styling
Shaving or trimming pubic hair, removing some but not all of it in a given style.
- Shaving - Head
Removing all traces of hair from the head.
- Showers - Brown
Defecating on another person.
- Showers - Golden
Urinating on another person.
- Speculums - Anal
Using a medical tool to dilate (stretch open) the entrance to the anus, providing access within.
- Speculums - Vaginal
Using a medical tool to dilate (stretch open) the entrance to the vagina, providing access within.
- Swapping (Partner)
Sex between two or more couples where members of each couple exchange partners and have sex with them.
- Voyeurism

Watching someone, often without their knowledge, in a situation with sexual connotations.

- Worship - Boot
  Worshiping the boots of another person.
- Worship - Bottom
  Worshiping the bottom of another person.
- Worship - Breast
  Worshiping the breasts of another person.
- Worship - Foot
  Worshiping the feet of another person.
- Worship - Genital
  Worshiping the genitals of another person.
- Worship - High Heel
  Worshiping the high-heeled shoes of another person.
- Wrestling
  Wrestling with another person, overpowering them or being overpowered.

Now that you have explored the different articles that can be incorporated into a BDSM contract, I encourage you to read through the contract templates first before deciding on the one that fits your situation. The templates are only there as a guide to help provide all partners a structured document. Remember to change/add/delete each one as needed.

Chapter 6: Simple D/s Contract

This contract can be used for male or female Dominant/submissives. Change the prepositions as needed to fit your situation. It is a basic contract that outlines what each person agrees to during the relationship. If using this contract, remember to add/change/delete any parts you wish to make it fit your own situation and needs.

I, [submissive], with a free mind and open heart; do request of [Dominant], that he accept the submission of my will unto him and take me into his care and guidance, that we may grow together in love, trust, and mutual respect. The satisfaction of his wants, desires, and whims are consistent with my desire as a submissive to be found pleasing to him. To that end, I offer him the use of my time, talents, and abilities.

Further, I ask, in sincere humility, that as my Dominant, he accept the keeping of my body, for the fulfillment and enhancement of our sexual, spiritual, emotional, and intellectual needs. To achieve this, he may have unfettered use of my body any time, any place, in front of anyone; to keep or give away as he will determine.

I ask that he guide any sexual, sensual, or scene-related behavior, both together with, and separate from him, in such a way as to further my growth as a person.

I request of [Dominant's name], that he/she use the power of his/her role to mold and shape me thus assisting me to grow as a total being in strength, character, and confidence.

In return, I agree:
- To obey his commands to the best of my ability
- To strive to overcome feelings of guilt or shame, and all inhibitions that interfere with my capability to serve him and limit my growth as his submissive
- To maintain honest and open communications with him

- To reveal my thoughts, feelings, and desires without hesitation or embarrassment
- To inform him of my wants and perceived needs, recognizing that he is the sole judge of whether or how these shall be satisfied
- To strive toward maintenance of a positive self-image and development of realistic expectations and goals
- To work with him to become a happy and self-fulfilled individual
- To work against negative aspects of my ego and my insecurities that would interfere with advancement of these aims

My surrender as a submissive is done with the knowledge that nothing asked of me will demean me as a person, and in no way diminish my own responsibilities toward making use of my potential.

This I, [submissive] do entreat, with lucidity and the realization of what this means, both stated and implied, in the conviction that this offer will be understood in the spirit of faith, caring, esteem, and devotion in which it is given.

Should either of us find that our aspirations are not being well served by this agreement, find this commitment too burdensome, or for any other reason wish to cancel, either may do so by verbal notification to the other, in keeping with the consensual nature of the agreement.

We both understand that cancellation means a cessation of the control stated and implied within this agreement, not a termination of our relationship as friends and lovers. Upon cancellation, each of us agrees to offer the other their reasons and assess our new needs and situation openly and lovingly.

This agreement shall serve as the basis for an extension of our relationship, committed to in the spirit of loving and consensual Dominance and submission with the intention of furthering self-awareness and exploration, promoting health and happiness, and improving both our lives.

This contract has a life of _____ (days/weeks/months/years). At its expiration a new contract may be created and signed.

I offer my consent of submission to [Dominant], under the terms stated above on this the _____ day of _____ in the year _____.

_____
(Signature of submissive)

I offer my acceptance of submission by [submissive], under the terms stated above on the _____ day of _____ in the year _____.

_____
(Signature of Dominant)

Chapter 7: Switch Couples' Contract

This contract provides a framework for consensual Switch BDSM play. By defining the boundaries of what is and is not to be included in the couples' sex play, overall satisfaction of both partners will be increased. Additional provisions under this contract may be added in a Contract Addendum. If using this contract, remember to add/change/delete any parts you wish to make it fit your own situation and needs. This contract can be used for male or female Dominant/submissives. Change the prepositions as needed to fit your situation.

General Agreement

Each partner will complete a punishment and limits form. The partners must agree to hold one or two sessions in each play cycle. In a single session only one partner assumes the dominant role and dispenses punishment as prescribed by the itemized list. A double session is split with roles reversed at an agreed upon time or point in the play.

Other considerations:
The session must be held at least once a week or every _____.

A refusal to submit at the appointed time will result in an additional six strokes for the refuser. If a dispute arises over an offense, it will be negotiated between the couple or an arbitrator may be appointed in an Addendum.

The Rules

The Rules are a list of offenses and the agreed upon punishment for each offense. Each offense will have a minimum and maximum number of strokes and a force level associated with it. The implement used and the actual number of strokes delivered in the punishment is at the discretion of the spanker. Both partners will write and maintain their own Rules list that clearly specifies what is expected of the other partner. Any items on the list must be accepted by the other partner before it becomes active. Acceptance is indicated by initialing and dating the item.

Punishment List
As each infraction of the Rules occurs, an entry is made on this form by the owner of the rule. The form may be used in formal review to set up the session or during the session as each item is meted out.

The undersigned agree to abide by all the above specified terms for a period of _____.

_____ Date:_____

_____ Date:_____

Chapter 8: Master/Slave Contract

This contract is used for an established, long-term live-in relationship. Before entering into this type of relationship, careful consideration must be given to how the submissive will be housed and supported financially by the Dominant. If the Dominant is asking the submissive to give up a job, then a legal contract, in addition to this contract, needs to be established by an attorney detailing money the dominant will give or allow the submissive, how health insurance for the submissive will be provided, as well as how much time and money the submissive will have if either party decides to end the relationship. As a dominant, you need to be able to provide for your submissive in a manner that they are accustomed to or better. If the submissive has separate real estate property, how that property will be maintained should also be included in a legal agreement.

If using this contract, remember to add/change/delete any parts you wish to make it fit your own situation and needs. This contract can be used for male or female Dominant/submissives. Change the prepositions as needed to fit your situation.

SLAVE CONTRACT BETWEEN

_____ AND _____

_____, herein after referred to as "Owner", hereby binds this contract with [his/her] signature and the signature of _____, herein after referred to as "slave" in this Submission Contract. Said Contract refers to total dominance and control of Owner in [his/her] relationship with said slave.

Purpose

The purpose of the servant contract is very important to instill the security of Ownership and all that such servitude implies. The contract is a measure of control. This contract is written to make clear the expectations of Owner and the consequences for failure to live up to this agreement. The contract is a reminder of the many duties and responsibilities of a live-in slave.

Symbols of Ownership include _____ upon signing this Contract, and any other future marks or tokens Owner may wish to bestow. Symbols of Ownership are visible reminders of status and should be worn with pride. They signify control and the lifestyle chosen by slave.

Duties of Servitude
(Add/Change/Delete as needed)

- Above all, it is the duty of the servant to please.
- Personal Duties: Physical/emotional needs of Owner, amusement, sexual toy/plaything, physical comfort, obedience, honesty, loyalty, waiting on Owner as desired and needed.
- Household Duties: Cleaning and keeping the home in order, laundry, shopping, cooking, care for children when requested, run errands as needed. Any task assigned is considered permanent.

Daily Routine
(Add/Change/Delete as needed)

The established daily routine includes:
• Arise 7-8am
• Morning coffee and breakfast
• Work
• Serving as Owner needs
• Household duties as needed
• Dinner duties
• Recreation with permission from Owner
• 11pm Bed-time

Recreation
(Add/Change/Delete as needed)

If slave wishes to enjoy the use of the computer [he/she] will ask for a
specific time [he/she] wishes to do so. Permission will be by grant of
Owner and slave will stop using the computer within 10 minutes after that
time set by Owner unless an extension is asked for and granted. If Owner
is not at home or unavailable, slave may be permitted to engage in this or
other recreation activities. Any chores, commands or cleaning that need
to be done will take preference over recreation activity except in the case
of a need for a break.

Expenditures
(Add/Change/Delete as needed)

All requests for major expenditures will be submitted to Owner for
approval. Any expenditure over $10.00 will be completely subject to the
approval of Owner prior to purchase unless said item may be returned for
a full refund.

Allowance
(Add/Change/Delete as needed)

Allowance will be set by Owner and distributed to slave as [he/she] sees
fit.

Exclusions
(Add/Change/Delete as needed)

Slave will be allowed _____ hours per day [or _____ days per week] for
time off, if requested in advance and if Owner agrees.

Owner will not injure, permanently scar or change any part of slave's
body unless slave gives written consent (tattoo/branding/piercing).

Stipulation

(Add/Change/Delete as needed)

Slave hereby acknowledges that Owner's authority supersedes [his/hers] in any decision including but not limited to travel plans, visitations, activities, chores, recreation, monetary expenses or expenditures, obligations, managements, diets, readings, processes, consumptions, priorities, communications or any otherwise alternative decision.

Owner will solely determine the residence, including city, county, state and/or country of residence for said slave.

Behavior
(Add/Change/Delete as needed)

- Attitude: The slave should show an attitude of respect at all times. Disrespect is a serious offense and will be punished severely.
- Respect includes: manner of speech, promptness, kneeling to serve, proper answers, obedience, loyalty and honesty.
- Respect and obedience are the two most important aspects of attitude the slave shall show at all times. Failure will be punished.

Friends and Relatives

All friends and relatives of Owner will be treated with the utmost respect. No anger, argument, condescension, criticism, insult or lack of courtesy will be tolerated. Owner will voice [his/her] compliment, respect and love for same at all times.

Slave hereby agrees to refrain from any insult or criticism of any of Owner's friends or relatives, their culture, attributes, background, class, heritage, or nationality, or any conceived notion detrimental to their status.

Owner may provide lodging for any friend, relative or partner [he/she] wishes. Permission is required from Owner if slave has the desire to provide lodging for any friend, relative or partner. Any disobedience from this rule will be the cause of serious punishment

Behavior in Private
(Add/Change/Delete as needed)

Slave shall address Owner as _____ at all times without fail. Slave shall pay full attention to Owner when spoken to.

Owner is more important than any other activity the slave may be engaged in. The slave shall sit, stand, walk, kneel, and lay where, when, and how Owner desires.

Slave shall stay in bed at night unless permission is granted to do otherwise. The slave shall not remove any restraint device for any other reason than an emergency.

Behavior in Public
(Add/Change/Delete as needed)

The slave shall address Owner as [Sir/Ma'am] at all times when there is not enough privacy to use the afore-mentioned title _____. The slave shall remain within eyesight of Owner unless permission is given to do otherwise. The slave shall be courteous and prompt at all times, showing Owner full respect.

The slave shall dress as Owner desires.

The slave shall not argue or complain when in public with Owner.

Training
(Add/Change/Delete as needed)

Training activities include: daily discipline, offering bed cuffs, proper answers, spending the night in bondage.

Slave will be given a weekly training scheduled for Friday night. Slave shall keep [his/her] Friday evenings free so as to have plenty of time for discipline training.

Discipline includes: bondage and restraint, leash training, implements of discipline, training, body and foot worship.

Punishment will be given for the following offenses:
(Add/Change/Delete as needed)

• Going anywhere without permission and/or threatening to do so
• Cockiness or rudeness
• Drinking without permission
• Disobedience

The slave shall perform the confession ritual once a month and be punished accordingly. Failure will be punished.

Explicit Permission: Slave will continually be trained and tested in explicit permission technique.

Special training activities include: Owner's complete control in [his/her] use of humiliation, surprise discipline, cage/bondage time, gags, hoods, etc., cleaning, servant feeding, retraining.

Progress Reports: Owner will prepare progress reports on the training of the slave as [he/she] desires.

Orgasm Control

Slave is to achieve orgasm ONLY by permission of Owner.

Slave's orgasms will be controlled for proper training of slave, teaching slave good habits, providing motivation, physical and sexual energy. Owner will allow slave reward upon permission.

Punishments
(Add/Change/Delete as needed)

• Mild Punishments can include: slapping, ear or nipple pinching, cropping, hair pulling, going to bed early, time-outs
• Medium Punishments can include: multiple slapping, genital pinching, intense bondage time, clamps and weights.
• Severe Punishments can include: panty or ball gags, leg chains and/or handcuffs, caning.

Drinking and Drugs
(Add/Change/Delete as needed)

Slave is allowed to drink alcohol or use _____ drugs only with explicit permission from Owner, when and where and how much [he/she] permits.

Drinking [will/will not] be permitted when going out to eat, [limited to 1 or 2 drinks with permission]. Slave may attend bars, etc., only with Owner, or with [his/her] permission to go with anyone else. Slave must ask permission for each and every drink.

Social Contact
(Add/Change/Delete as needed)

Slave is allowed to write, visit and talk to any family member as long as it does not interfere with [his/her] servitude.

Slave is allowed to write, visit and talk to friends as long as it does not interfere with [his/her] servitude. All such contact will be monitored by Owner.

These are privileges, not rights, and should be appreciated.

Duration

This Contract is valid from this day until 6 months has passed, and then it may be renewed or renegotiated if Owner and/or slave feel it needs to be reviewed and updated. At that time, the slave will receive a new contract.

Accepted, understood and agreed to

this _____ day of _____, 20__:

By:

_____, Owner

_____, slave

Chapter 9: Scene Only Contract

This is to be used in a scene or play session only situation. Note that as much detail as you can provide should be filled in to ensure all parties in the scene are on the same page. If using this contract, remember to add/change/delete any parts you wish to make it fit your own situation and needs. This contract can be used for male or female Dominant/submissives. Change the prepositions as needed to fit your situation.

The following person(s) will participate in the session:

_____
_____
_____
_____
_____

Note: The session will involve only those persons specifically named above. One copy of this form will be completed by each of the participants named above and a copy filed along with two copies of legal proof of age identification.

The session will begin at ____ : ____ am pm ____ _____ , 20 ___ , or as soon thereafter as all participants are assembled, ready and all necessary preparations are complete.

Estimated Duration: _____
Start Signal: _____
End Signal: _____
The session will end at or not later than ____ : ____ am pm ____
_____ , ___

Type of scene(s) to be enacted:

• Master / slave Dom

- Mistress / slave FemDom
- Servant Butler, Maid, Lawn Boy, Secretary
- Captivation Abduction, Penal
- Forced Rape, Blackmail
- Gender Play Cross Dressing, TV
- Age Play Diapers, School, Geriatric
- Animal Play Pony, Domestication
- Other:

_____

The following list of Hard Limits shall not be pushed or breached:

_____
_____
_____
_____
_____

SAFEWORDS:

_____ when used means all is OK to proceed.
_____ when used means submissive needs to slow down some or talk about what is happening at that moment.
_____ when used means ALL STOP IMMEDIATELY.

In testament by signature below, we the undersigned BDSM Session Participants (the Participants) agree to the terms and limitations established by this Contract. No change shall be made during the Session unless noted in amendment to this Contract prior to said change being enacted.

The Participants do hereby certify that this Agreement is being executed by their own freewill without promise, threat or coercion in any form.

The Participants do hereby certify that this Agreement is being executed with full prior knowledge of the potential for physical, psychological and / or legal hazard and agree to hold blameless and without fault all other Participants for the same excepting where said
Participants willfully engage in actions or activities in violation of the terms and limitations set forth by this Agreement.

The Participants do hereby certify that they are above the legal age of consent for the jurisdiction in which this Agreement and Session are executed and have faithfully provided proof of the same as attached hereto.

If any court determines that any provision of this Agreement is invalid or unenforceable, any invalidity or unenforceability will affect only that provision and will not make any other provision of this Agreement invalid or unenforceable and such provision shall be modified, amended or limited only to the extent necessary to render it valid and enforceable.

The Participants do hereby certify that they know of no legal or other impediment that would prevent them from fully and completely entering into this Agreement and Contract and hereby so do on this ___ day of

_____, ____ .

Participants:

_____ Date:_____

_____ Date:_____

Chapter 10: Online Only Relationship Contract

The purpose of this contract is for Online Only Relationships (D/s, M/s, DD/lg). Since every online only relationship has extremely different circumstances, I have provided a blank framework that needs to be filled in with your specific rules/needs/protocols/etc. This contract can be used for male or female Dominant/submissives. Change the prepositions as needed to fit your situation. If using this contract, remember to add/change/delete any parts you wish to make it fit your own situation and needs.

I, [Dominant] known as the Dominant, do request of [submissive] known as the submissive:
1. Rules
2. Tasks (Daily or Weekly)
3. Clothing options
4. Check-ins and GPS tracking
5. Special Body Grooming
6. Detailed Daily routine

I, [submissive], with a free mind and open heart; do request of [Dominant],
1. Fill in any requests here you want the Dominant to adhere to
2. During the length of your relationship.
3.
4.
5.
6.

Dominant's Limits: (Fill in below)
1.
2.
3.
4.

5.

Submissive's Limits: (Fill in below)

    1.
    2.
    3.
    4.
    5.

The duration of this contract shall be valid for (List length of time) from (list start date).

Accepted, understood and agreed to

this _____ day of _____, 20__:

By:

_____, Dominant (Name)

_____, submissive (Name)

About the Author:

I have been in and around the BDSM Lifestyle for over 20 years as a submissive/slave. I mentor and advise new people, as well as write educational books and blogs on different subjects from a submissive point of view. I share my own life experiences and incites in hopes of inspiring others.

I have accumulated many diverse skills over the course of my employment history. Currently, I utilize skills as a writer, researcher, strategist, creative thinker and mentor on a daily basis. I have the ability to think creatively and come up with innovative solutions to different problems or challenges.

I strive to help educate and guide people about the real world of BDSM. It is a beautiful and most often misunderstood Lifestyle. My goal is to give correct information versus the distorted / incorrect news / reports about our Lifestyle.

My partner and I are dedicated to spreading the knowledge of BDSM by publishing books and articles on the web, where we have a significant presence. Many people contact us asking for relational - emotional advice. Sometimes they need qualified professional help. In these cases, I would be able to suggest a professional therapist.

I would like to grow my opportunities and accept connections that can assist in expanding our mutual networks. Feel free to connect with me at michellefegatofi@gmail.com.

I hope you found this book a useful tool in your journey to your own BDSM journey.

Please leave a review of the book on the site that you purchased it from. Reviews are not only helpful to author for future works, but also help other would be readers.

www.ingramcontent.com/pod-product-compliance
Lightning Source LLC
Chambersburg PA
CBHW020405290526
45785CB00005B/2449